BACKYARD SAFARI

Bats

Wil Mara

Cavendish
Square

New York

Published in 2014 by Cavendish Square Publishing, LLC
303 Park Avenue South, Suite 1247, New York, NY 10010

Website: cavendishsq.com

Library of Congress Cataloging-in-Publication Data

Mara, Wil.
Bats / by Wil Mara.
p. cm. — (Backyard safari)
Includes index.
ISBN 978-1-62712-295-5 (hardcover) ISBN 978-1-62712-296-2 (paperback) ISBN 978-1-62712-297-9 (ebook)
1. Bats — Juvenile literature. I. Mara, Wil. II. Title.
QL737.C5 M28 2014
599.4—dc23

Editorial Director: Dean Miller
Senior Editor: Peter Mavrikis
Copy Editor: Cynthia Roby
Art Director: Jeffrey Talbot
Designer: Joseph Macri
Photo Researcher: Alison Morretta
Production Manager: Jennifer Ryder-Talbot
Production Editor: Andrew Coddington

The photographs in this book are used by permission and through the courtesy of: Cover photo by Art Wolfe/Iconica/Getty Images; Paul Kennedy/Lonely Planet Images/Getty Images, 4; Jack Milchanowski/age footstock/Getty Images, 5; Ivan Kuzmin/imagebrok / imagebroker.net /SuperStock, 6; National Geographic / SuperStock, 8; Minden Pictures /SuperStock, 9; WIN-Initiative/WIN-Initiative/Getty Images, 11; Photo Researchers/Photo Researchers/Getty Images, 12; Minden Pictures / SuperStock, 15; Visuals Unlimited, Inc./Joe McDonald/Visuals Unlimited/Getty Images, 17; Enzo Tomasiello/Stringer/Getty Images News/Getty Images, 18; Mark Carwardine/Peter Arnold/Getty Images, 21; Alvin E Staffan/Photo Researchers/Getty Images, 22; Gary Retherford/ Photo Researchers/Getty Images, 22; Jared Hobbs/All Canada Photos/Getty Images, 22; M Burnley John/Photo Researchers/Getty Images, 22; Biosphoto / SuperStock, 23; Biosphoto / SuperStock, 25; Biosphoto / SuperStock, 26; Stockbyte/Stockbyte/Getty Images, 27.

Printed in the United States of America

Contents

Introduction

Have you ever watched a squirrel chasing another squirrel around a tree? Or a group of deer leaping gracefully through a stretch of winter woods? If you have, then you know how wonderful it is to discover nature for yourself. Each book in the Backyard Safari series takes you step-by-step on an easy outdoor adventure, and then helps you identify the animals you've found. You'll also learn ways to attract, observe, and protect these valuable creatures. As you read, be on the lookout for the Safari Tips and Trek Talk facts sprinkled throughout the book. Ready? The fun starts just steps from your back door!

ONE
A Bat's Life

Bat Bodies

It's easy to think of bats as birds, as they look like them and tend to, well, fly around a lot. But bats are actually **mammals**—which mean they're related to you! They are, in fact, the only mammals capable of flying in the true sense. You may have heard about other "flying" mammals such as flying squirrels or gliding possums, but they can only float through the air for short distances, which isn't the same as actual flight. Bats fly with the help of their "wings," which are really hands with very long and narrow fingers and flaps of skin between them. Bat wings are different from bird wings because a bat's has no feathers! The surface of a bat's wings is sensitive to touch, much in the same way as your fingers. Bat wings also have millions

Bats are the only mammals that can truly fly. Their "wings" are really more like hands with long, webbed fingers.

of tiny hairs, giving them even greater sensitivity. This is very helpful to a bat when it is flying or trying to capture **prey**.

Bats' eyes are very small in relation to the rest of their heads. In spite of what you may have heard, however, bats are not blind.

Most bats have tiny eyes in relation to their heads, an upturned snout that often resembles that of a pig, and ears that sometimes appear ridiculously large and pointy. The ears, however, are among the most important part of its body, as you will soon learn. A bat's body is covered with fine fur that can range in color from light brown or tan to a dark black. Most bats grow to about 3 to 6 inches (8 to 15 cm) in length, which is average for their bodies. The smallest **species** of bat is the Kitti's hog-nosed bat, also known as the bumblebee bat. Its body size averages a little over 1 inch (3 cm). This bat can be found in limestone caves along rivers of western Thailand and southeast Burma. Among the largest species of bat is the golden-crowned flying fox. Found only in the Philippines, it can grow to nearly a full foot (30 cm) and weigh up to 4 pounds (1.81 kg).

Here, There, and Everywhere

Bats are found all over the world in every area except a few small islands and anywhere near the North or South poles. They are very adaptable, meaning they can survive under all sorts of conditions, and therefore live in a broad variety of environments. There are bats in and around tropical forests, dry deserts, murky swamps, clear lakes, swirling oceans, crowded farmlands, busy suburbs, and even busier cities. Some species will even migrate, or travel to different **habitats**, depending on the time of year. What they need most of all are places to hide (which are called **roosts**) during the day and plenty of opportunities to feed when it gets dark. So, put very simply, bats are just about everywhere—which is good news for you as you prepare for your safari!

Bats usually rest during the day and then come out just after the sun has set.

Days and Nights

Bats are nocturnal, meaning they are creatures of the night. Most species are particularly active during **twilight** hours—when the sun is no longer visible on the horizon but is still giving off light. Usually bats respond to twilight in the evening when the sun goes down, rather than just before it comes up in the morning. After that, they can be out searching for food at any time during the night. Part of the reason for this is that most birds hunt during the day, so bats don't have to compete with them for food at night. The majority of bat species—about 70 percent—eat insects. Of the remaining 30 percent, most feed on fruits. A few will eat small animals such as fish and small birds, and in some cases, other smaller bats. But, in spite of the popular belief that bats are "vampires" that feed on blood, the truth is that only a handful of species actually do this.

Bats hunt through means of **echolocation**, which is complex system of making sounds, having those sounds bounce back, and then forming images in their brains as to what's around them. Those sounds are so high-pitched that humans cannot hear them. Bats are incredibly efficient at finding things to eat or getting around obstacles while flying at remarkable speeds. Some species can fly at speeds of more than 60 miles per hour. And although you may be under the impression that bats need

Most bats eat insects, and a smaller percentage feed on fruits.
A few species, including the vampire bat, feed on blood.

echolocation because they can't see (as in the phrase, "blind as a bat"), the truth is that all bats can see. Many of them can see really well, even in light that is not too bright. And while their sense of hearing is obviously excellent, they also have a well-developed sense of smell.

Trek Talk
You won't see bats on a rainy day because the rain interferes with their echolocation, plus there aren't as many prey items to find. Also, the water weighs down their wings and makes it harder for them to fly. Remember all this when you go on your bat safari—rainy days are not best for bat watching!

Breeding

Bat mothers usually have their babies in the spring, following a period of long rest. In warmer areas, this rest period is known as **torpor**, but in colder parts of the world they will undergo true hibernation. Female bats can have more than one birth during a single season. She may have just one birth if she senses that there is not enough food available. Most bats will have just one baby (known as a "**pup**") at a time, and the mother will care for it until it reaches adulthood. Newborn bats have to wait anywhere from six weeks to four months before they're able to fly on their own, depending on the species. The average lifespan for a bat in the wild is anywhere from 16 to 20 years.

A bat will not be able to fly for about a month after birth. In the meantime, its mother will make sure it is well fed.

TWO
You Are the Explorer

As we have already learned, bats are most active during "twilight" hours—when the sun is just about to rise or has just come down (usually the second one) and there is still light in the sky. They are also active during the night, but it's much harder to see them! The best time of the year to look for bats is during the warmer months, particularly in the spring after they've come out of hibernation and need to eat a lot in order to get their body weight back up.

Bats are not solitary animals and are often found in huge groups of hundreds or even thousands.

What Do I Wear?

* Old clothes that can get dirty or torn
* Clothes that are also loose-fitting and comfortable
* Any type of shoes will do, but if you're going to venture into the woods, wear something durable like a pair of boots
* You can wear a hat if you wish, but the old story about bats flying into people's hair and becoming tangled is not true
* Bug spray

What Do I Take?

* Binoculars
* Digital camera
* Notebook
* Pen or pencil
* Cell phone
* A folding chair
* A snack for yourself

Where Do I Go?

To find bats during their active hours, you need to go to where their food is, because that's where they'll be. Since most North American species eat insects, these are the best places to find bats hunting them:

❄ Near bodies of water, such as streams, rivers, lakes, and ponds. Still water (as opposed to moving water) is best. You can even go to a large puddle after a heavy rainstorm, provided that the puddle has been sitting awhile and bugs have had the chance to notice it.

❄ In a meadow, grassy field, etc. Insects love these places and will gather there by the thousands.

❄ Lawns, shrubs, and other landscaping. Yes, bats will come right into your backyard—provided you have the kind of environment where insects like to gather.

❄ Around bright lights. Bugs *love* to fly around lights during dusk and night hours. They are attracted not just to the brightness but also the warmth—and bats know this. Pay particular attention to streetlamps, which are high up and therefore easier for bats to access.

❄ Wherever bats are roosting. It's not easy to locate a spot where you know for sure that bats roost during the day. This can be any number of places, including inside the cracks of an old house, in an abandoned building, a cave, and inside a hollow tree. Bats won't necessarily hunt right around their roosting sites, either. But if you do know of a roost, you will at the very least be able to see the bats come out when the time is right. It can be a very interesting sight.

It's very important to remember that you should always be with an adult that you trust when you go on your bat safari. It can be very risky for a youngster such as yourself to walk around when it's dark out, so don't do it alone. Also, if you go on someone else's property, make sure you have permission to do so. You can get into a lot of trouble for trespassing.

Bats need to drink like most any other animal, and they can often be seen flying around ponds and lakes.

What Do I Do?

❋ Be patient. This is the most important thing to do on your bat safari, because you might not see a hundred bats during the first five minutes. Remember, they don't just hunt in one spot—they hunt all over the place! That means they could be all around your neighborhood, just not where you're standing. If there are a lot of insects flying around, the bats will come!

❋ Keep still and quiet. We have already learned that bats don't attack people. Even if one swoops down to where you're standing, it is most likely because it sensed an insect nearby or even the heat from your body. But if you move around a lot and make noise, you will distract the bats and may even frighten them off. Many bat watchers like to bring along a folding chair so they'll be comfortable during the wait. (There's no real advantage to standing up anyway, so why not?) This is also the reason that you'll want to bring along a snack—in case you get hungry!

❋ Listen carefully. Bats make noise. You really can't hear the high-pitched squeals they emit during echolocation—that's on a frequency generally undetectable by humans—but they do flap their wings, and they do cut through the air at great speeds.

Safari Tip

If you're near a body of water, watch the water from time to time, too. Bats do need to drink, and it's a pretty interesting thing to see. When thirsty, bats swoop down just over the water's surface, stick their tongues out, and lap it up like a dog. They have also been known to lick droplets. They'll usually drink within the first hour after emerging from their roost—something to remember if you go on your safari just as the sun goes down.

On an otherwise calm night, these are the sounds you should be able to hear. If you're near a roosting site—which usually has dozens or even hundreds of bats inside—you should bc able to hear them clicking and clawing inside as they're getting ready to leave for the hunt.

Pay close attention to the skies around you. Bats can be seen in the night sky—but only if you're watching carefully. Don't forget that they can fly at speeds up to 60 miles per hour. Sometimes they will appear as little more than a blur, as bats will enter your field of vision, zoom by, and then disappear again. They're not like birds in that they'll land, hang around awhile, and then lift lazily away. They are always on the move, so you have to be alert at all times.

Some people are afraid of bats, but the truth is they help us by eating millions of pesky insects.

❋ Keep your camera ready. You can get pictures of bats, but you will need a bit of luck. Make sure your camera is always ready and that the flash is on. Some bat watchers will simply shoot frame after frame when they see a bat and hope they got at least one or two good shots. Whatever methods you try, don't get discouraged if you don't come away with any award-winning photos. Bats are very uncooperative subjects!

❋ When you do see a bat, make notes in your notebook. What did it look like? How big was it? Where were you when you saw it? From what direction did it fly? (This information could be helpful in backtracking to a roosting site.) Was there more than one bat? If so, how many? And what time did you see them? Was it the same time as the night before? After you gather enough data, you might begin to see patterns emerge that will help you with future safaris.

❋ When you return home, download any pictures you took, and show them to your friends and family. You could also write a more formal journal, using both the pictures you took and the notes you made. You could keep an ongoing record of your bat safaris from year to year.

THREE
A Guide to Bats

There are many different bat species in North America, so figuring out which ones you've seen on your safari could be a challenge. Still, some species are very common and widespread, whereas others are quite rare. Let's give identification a shot.

❋ First, get your notes you scribbled down while you were "in the field" along with those great pictures you took (if you were lucky enough to get any). Next, read through your notes and ask the following questions:

❋ What was the bat's overall color?

❋ What was the color of its wings, legs, ears, and snout? Sometimes these colors can be different from the rest of the body.

❋ How big was the bat?

❋ How big were the bat's ears in relation to the rest of its body?

❋ Was the bat flying alone or with other bats? If with others, about how many?

Bats use their claws to hold on and hang upside down from branches.

Now, go to the next page and see if any of the bats in the photos match up with the **characteristics** that you noted in your answers. Although there are many bat species in North America, a lot of them look similar from a distance. This can make them hard to identify. But even if you have trouble, don't get discouraged. Sometimes you can use other information—such as your location (town, state, country) or the exact habitat in which you saw them—to provide the final pieces of your puzzle. Doing a little research on the Internet should also help. Further resources are provided for you in this book's Find Out More section.

Silver-haired Bat

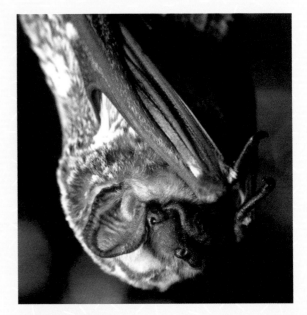

Hoary Bat

Big Brown Bat

Little Brown Bat

FOUR

Try This!
Projects You Can Do

Bats fly in the sky, and the rest of the time they hide, so it might be easy to get the impression they don't interact with people very much. But that doesn't mean you still can't undertake a few fun bat projects. Just because you won't be sitting in your living room with a bat on your lap, as you would a dog or cat, doesn't mean you can't help them out.

A bat's favorite place to roost is in a cave.

The Bug Trap

Nobody likes bugs, right? Well, bats do…but *you* probably don't. Bugs can bite, sting, carry all sorts of illnesses, scare you, and all sorts of unpleasant things. But bats love them! So here's a way to make both you and your local bats very happy. Cut the top off a large plastic soda bottle, punch two holes in either side of the top that remains (i.e., what used to be the bottle's "sides"), and then attach a piece of string so the bottle can be hung. Then, put a little "fly bait" into the bottle—raw meat or old fruit should work. Now, hang the bottle outside somewhere (preferably away from your house) during the night and shine a light on it. Between the light and the bait, flying insects should come along by the thousands. And once they do, the bats won't be long behind them. If you set this up just right, you can watch for bats in the comfort of your own home. (You could even set up a camera.) Not only will you make the bats happy, you'll get rid of a lot of flying pests in your area.

Build-a-Roost

As interesting as bats are, you certainly don't want them living in your house! However, if you have a little land on your property, you can put together a simple roosting spot that's close by. You'll need an adult to help, as there will probably be some woodcutting involved. Basically, you

Bat Rescue

If you suspect bats have taken up residence in your home, the most important first step you need to remember is not to panic. Bats wiggle their way into outside cracks and crevices in people's homes all the time. They don't

burrow or chew their way in, they simply enter openings that are already there. And don't be afraid, because they're not there to attack you in your sleep or grab your parents and fly off with them. All they're looking for is a place to rest during the day. Sometimes people who discover bats in their homes have the urge to fill in whatever hole the bats are using. That's a very bad idea because the bats will panic and then look for other ways to get out. This usually results in having them fly around your house. You don't need to do anything more than call an animal control service (there are lots of them these days) and let them take care of the problem. Out of kindness, make sure you use a service that will catch and move the bats to another location rather than destroy them.

Bats will likely use this roost to rest during the day. Make sure not to disturb them!

want to end up with a box that you can attach to a tree or something similar. It has to be roughly square in shape, but with very little depth (two or three inches will be plenty). Here's the important part: the top and sides should be enclosed, but the bottom should be left open. This is where the bats will fly in and out. Attach some netting to the inside walls so the bats can "hang out" on it. It may take awhile for your local bats to discover the roost, but once they do, they'll probably use it for years to come. And try to resist the urge to "check on them" a lot. If you bother them too much, they may leave and go use someone else's roost!

The Echolocation Game

Would you like to hunt the same way bats do? It's not easy, but it can be fun and educational. It'll also give you a much greater appreciation for what bats have to do in order to get a meal every night! You and a few friends need to stand in your backyard or some other open place.

The Echolocation Game gives you a chance to feel what it's like to be a live bat.

One of you takes on the role of "the bat," and the others will be the "bugs." The bat should either close his eyes or wear a blindfold. The bat calls out "echo" while the bugs call back "location." Then the bat has to find the bugs with only his hearing. It's okay for the bugs to move around during the game, because that's what real bugs do when bats are hunting them! As soon as the bat "tags" a bug, that bug has been eaten and is out of the game. See how long it takes to get them all.

Trek Talk

If you ever do get close to a wild bat, resist the urge to trap it. Bats frighten easily and do not like being touched or held. Some bats do carry diseases that will make you sick, but even those that don't can deliver nasty bites and scratches. If you come across a bat that doesn't try to move away from you, chances are it is sick and therefore definitely should not be touched. Have an adult put the bat in a box (make sure they have on a pair of gloves), then call an animal control service or a local zoo to remove it.

Glossary

characteristic   a specific trait or quality that an animal has, such as tan fur or brown eyes

echolocation   the practice of making sounds, having them bounce off objects, and then using the bounced-back sounds to form mental pictures of what's nearby

habitat   the exact type of place in which an animal lives, such as a burrow, cave, or shoreline

hibernate   a period of deep rest that many animals go into during cold months

mammal   any vertebrate animal (one that has a backbone) belonging to the class known as Mammalia. Mammals are covered in hair or fur, and nurse their babies on mother's milk.

prey   any animal that is hunted by another

pup   a newborn bat

roost   a place where a bat rests during the day

species   one particular type of animal

torpor   a long period of rest similar to hibernation, but not as deep

twilight   time of day when the sun is below the horizon but still giving off light

Find Out More

Books

Carson, Mary Kay. *The Bat Scientists*. San Anselmo, CA: Sandpiper Press, 2013.

Rodriguez, Ana Maria. *Vampire Bats, Giant Insects, and Other Mysterious Animals of the Darkest Caves*. Berkeley Heights, NJ: Enslow Publishers, 2012.

Zeiger, Jennifer. *Bats*. New York: Children's Press, 2013.

Websites

Bats for Kids

www.bats4kids.org/

This website has answers to many of the most commonly asked questions from kids about bats. You will also find fun projects, games, and quizzes.

All Things Bats

www.kidzone.ws/animals/bats/

The KidZone page for bats has facts, photos, and a large selection of fun activities including games and drawings that can be printed for coloring.

Incredible Bats

www.incrediblebats.com/interactive.html

This website has strong visual content that includes lots of great photos and videos, plus an amazing variety of bat-related games, news, facts, links, and other resources.

Index

Page numbers in **boldface** are illustrations.

About the Author

WIL MARA is an award-winning author of more than 140 books. He began his writing career with several titles about herpetology, or, the study of reptiles and amphibians. He has since branched out into other subject areas and continued to write educational books for children. To find out more about Mara and his work, you can visit his website at www.wilmara.com.